I0166835

In Less Than 10 Minutes

Beatrice Holloway

TSL Drama

First published in Great Britain in 2018
By TSL Publications, Rickmansworth

Copyright © 2018 Beatrice Holloway

ISBN / 978-1-912416-13-4

Image courtesy of : https://pixabay.com/en/sparrows-parents-feeding-family-2426763/

The right of Beatrice Holloway to be identified as the playwright/ author of this work has been asserted by the author in accordance with the UK Copyright, Designs and Patents Act 1988.

All characters and events in this publication, other than those clearly in the public domain, are fictitious and any resemblance to actual persons, living or dead, is purely coincidental.

All rights reserved. No part of this publication may be reproduced, stored in a retrieval system or transmitted, in any form or by any means without the prior written permission of the publisher, nor be otherwise circulated in any form of binding or cover other than that in which it is published and without a similar condition being imposed on the subsequent buyer.

Rights of performance

Rights of performance for this play is controlled by TSL Publications (tslbooks.uk/Drama) which issues a performing licence on payment of a fee and subject to a number of conditions (specified on tslbooks.uk/Drama). This play is fully protected under the Copyright Laws of the British Commonwealth of Nations, the United States of America and all countries of the Berne and Universal Copyright Conventions. All rights, including stage, Motion Picture, Radio, Television, Public Reading and Translation into Foreign Languages are strictly reserved. It is an infringement of the Copyright to give any performance or public reading of this play before the fee has been paid and the licence issued. The Royalty Fee is subject to contract and subject to variation at the sole discretion of TSL Publications. In Territories Overseas the fees quoted may not apply. A fee will be quoted on application to TSL Publications.

Dedication

so many, alongside the performers,
to thank for such marvellous entertainment.

In Less Than 10 Minutes

Characters

KATE	*Early 20s, married, mother of John's children*
JOHN	*Older than Kate, **wants to improve his education** and a little insensitive*
LOUISE	*Older than Kate, carefree nature*
EMILY	*A smart woman, 60ish*

Running Time

35-40 minutes

Scenes

Scene 1   Kate is busy and is frustrated by John's enthusiasm for poetry and the lecturer, Emily, thoughtlessly praising her.

Scene 2   Kate discusses her concerns about John's interest in Emily, with Louise. She is determined to do something about it, but Louise cautions her to be careful.

Scene 3   Louise is shocked when Kate reveals what she has done. John brings Emily home to introduce her to Kate, and the three realise there has been a case of mistaken identity.

Setting

John and Kate's sitting room with evidence of children all aged under five.

Wine rack with selection of wines.

Cabinet with wine and other glasses.

Dining table and chairs.

Scene 1

Lights up.

JOHN *and* KATE*'s sitting room where there is evidence of children toys, laundry etc scattered about.*

It is evening time and JOHN *is sitting at the table reading with a few open books in front of him.*

KATE *enters with a full laundry basket and proceeds to hang the children's clothing onto a clothes horse.*

KATE: Are you going to your meeting tonight or not?

JOHN: Yes, yes, just finishing this poem. Listen.
(*Reads tenderly.*) 'Strange that the urgent will in me, to set my mouth on hers in kisses,
And so softly to bring together two strange sparks, beget another life from our lives.'

KATE: (*Sarcastically.*) Yes dear. Very nice. Written by a man of course. Sparks he says, never heard it called that before.

JOHN: (*Exasperated.*) Nice! Is that all you can say. Nice!

I'll have you know it's one of the loveliest poems ever written as far as I'm concerned. It's called *Rose of all the World*. Just listen carefully to this bit. 'The innermost fire of my own dim soul out-spinning and whirling in blossom of flames and being upon me.'

KATE: Well, yes I suppose so, but a bit over the top innit? Sounds like he's got the hots. (*Pause.*) And I bet that

	was written before the poor cow had three kids. Who wrote it anyway?
JOHN:	DH Lawrence wrote it. Poetry has soul.
	(*Pause.*) 'Course it's better when she reads it.
KATE:	Oh you mean Miss Shakespeare. (*Mutters.*) I can just imagine.
JOHN:	You sound down in the dumps my girl. You need some time off yourself I'm thinking. (*Brightly.*) Tell you what. Why don't you and Lou join something? Take yourselves off one evening.
KATE:	Like what?
JOHN:	I don't know. (*Pause.*) Like ... Line dancing or Yoga or something girlie you both like.
	(*Looks around the room.*) Where's my jacket?
KATE:	Where you left it. (*Mimics him.*) Something girlie! (*Does exaggerated line dance steps.*)
	We've got brains too you know. (*Pause.*) Something girlie ye Gods!
	(*Does suggestive yoga pose.*) Like this?
JOHN:	(*Laughs. Goes across to her. Puts his finger under her chin.*) Kate, Kate. I love you.
	(*Begins romantically.*) How do I love thee? Let me count the ways.
	(*Pause. Counts on fingers.*) You are the mother of my children; (*Pause.*) you are a damn good cook AND (*Pause.*)
KATE:	(*Warns him.*) Be careful.
JOHN:	And fantastic in bed! (KATE *playfully slaps him. They both laugh. There is a knock on the door. JOHN picks up his coat and some books and opens the door.*) Right, I'm off! And how's my favourite sister-in-law?

LOUISE:	(*Puts up her face for air kiss from* JOHN *who leaves. Cheerfully.*) How's my lovely sister and her down-trodden housewife life?
KATE:	Shut up you, and welcome.
LOUISE:	(*Produces a bottle of wine.*) Come on come on, where's the glasses?
	KATE *gets glasses.*
	LOUISE *pours them a glass each.*
	They both bounce down onto the sofa. Each take a sip of wine.
	KATE *swallows half down quickly.*
LOUISE:	Everything alright?
KATE:	At the moment!
LOUISE:	Good, cos I'm just bursting to tell you the latest.
KATE:	Go on then. Who's done what to whom?
LOUISE:	Remember I told you about the new guy?
KATE:	Er? Robert something wasn't it. You fancied him like mad.
LOUISE:	Robin. Yes I did fancy him a bit.
KATE:	Honestly Lou! Why aren't you satisfied with George?
LOUISE:	George! 'Course I'm satisfied with good old George. (*Pause. Sighs.*) If only he was a bit more ... you know ... exciting.
KATE:	He's a good bloke. Solid, dependable someone you can trust.
LOUISE:	Exactly!
	KATE *drains her glass. Walks slowly about the room generally tidying up.*
KATE:	Well, I should grab him if I were you. Time you got wed and settled down.

LOUISE:	(*Horrified, squeaks out.*) Good God, you sounded just like mother then. (*Pause.*) I expect we will one day, but I do like the odd date with other guys.
KATE:	You what!
LOUISE:	Oh don't get alarmed. I haven't met one yet better than George, but I must tell you about Robin.
	(*Fills up the glasses.*) Got any crisps or something to go down with this wine?
KATE:	Probably, I'll just check. Won't be a mo.
	KATE *leaves the stage.*
	LOUISE *wanders about the room. Opens the book John left on the table.*
	KATE *returns.*
KATE:	Sorry, all I could find was the kids' jammy dodgers.
LOUISE:	They'll do fine.
	Both sit down. Take a biscuit and sip at their drinks.
	LOUISE *thumbs through book.*
LOUISE:	Is John really serious about this poetry lark?
KATE:	I'm not sure. He seems to be enjoying it. (*Laughs.*) He says he doesn't want to be a carpenter all his life so he's trying to improve himself.
LOUISE:	Yeh! But is he really enjoying it?
KATE:	(*Waspishly.*) He certainly seems to be enjoying something. (*Pause.*) So what was you saying about Robin? Abandoned you I suspect for someone cleverer no doubt.
LOUISE:	No! No! I reckon I was the clever one this time. It's the other three in my team that were idiots. Belinda, remember her?
KATE:	Who could forget! Blonde, tall and leggy, skirts around her backside. (*Mutters.*) I hate her.
LOUISE:	What? Oh never mind. Then there's Maggie.

KATE:	I like her. Came across as a bit shy, not too sure of herself.
LOUISE:	Shy, my eye! Not according to … And we mustn't leave out Ella. Supposed to be getting married next month.
KATE:	So what's the big crisis? (*Sees a child's vest has fallen off the clothes horse. She goes to pick it up. Smoothes it two or three times lovingly and rehangs it.*)
LOUISE:	(*Talks while* KATE *sorts laundry.*) Seems that rat Robin has dated all three of them these last two months. (*Stretches out her legs and takes another biscuit.*) 'Course none of them knew what was going on, so I suppose they've got some sort of excuse.
KATE:	(*Returns to sofa, picking up a cuddly toy. Takes it with her and sits nursing it.*) Excuse for what?
LOUISE:	Being stupid.
KATE:	Come on. Bet he turns out married!
LOUISE:	Oh boy! And how.
KATE:	So he turns out to be the usual office male shit.
LOUISE:	But that's not all. (*Holds up glass.*) Want another?
KATE:	No thanks. Listen did you hear something then?
LOUISE:	No. Like what?
KATE:	I thought I heard one of the kids.
LOUISE:	I don't think so. Hey, let me tell you. We'll listen out for them.
	Okay? Where was I? (*Pause.*) Yes, I was just about to tell you about yesterday.
KATE:	(*Moves to doorway.*) I was sure I heard something then.
	(*Pause.*) No. It seems to be all quiet. (*Returns to seat still cuddling toy.*)

LOUISE:	(*Takes a deep breath.*) Yesterday, we were all working frantically to get the end of month accounts finished, when someone barged into our office. She glared at all of us then stomped into Robin's office. I tell you we all stopped working. Belinda said, something like 'What the hell is going on?' and I thought Maggie was going to faint. She went so white.
KATE:	Mmm. (*Absentmindedly kisses the top of the toy's head and clutches it close to her.*)
LOUISE:	And then the fireworks began! She began slinging things around the office. I saw Robin duck when his coffee cup was aimed at him. She was screaming and shouting like a banshee and he ... just let her get on with it. Mind I could see he was sweating.
	I expect he thought the boss would come in in the middle of it all.
KATE:	And did he?
LOUISE:	Later on he did. After someone told him the computer had gone through the window! Got the sack on the spot.
KATE:	Serves him right.
LOUISE:	Then she came out and turned on us. 'What you all staring at you tarts. Yes tarts everyone of you.' Well Belinda went quite red and Ella told her she wasn't as she was getting married. So Mrs Robin screamed that she hoped Ella's husband would treat her better than hers!
KATE:	(*Solemnly.*) Hell hath no fury like a woman scorned.
LOUISE:	What! Oh listen. She went on to call us a few awful names like prostitutes and gold diggers, husband stealers and worse. Poor old Maggie began to cry. Well that did it. Mrs R turned on her. 'What you got to cry about? I suppose you shagged him like the

rest of them here.' Well the other two protested –
too much if you ask me.

KATE: Did they?

LOUISE: What?

KATE: You know, (*Leering at her sister.*) make lurve!

LOUISE: Don't know really. But I would guess so. Anyway Mrs R still bawling at poor old Maggie told her to thank her lucky stars she wasn't pregnant. 'Like me. Up the duff. In the pudding club, call it what you like but it's his third' she yelled. Then she begins to cry and we all begin to feel sorry for her. Mr R came out of his office and put his arm around her and whispered something. If looks could kill, I tell you that man would have dropped dead there and then. Then they both left thank God.

KATE: Well, one good thing about being a stay at home mum is missing out on the office politics. Honestly, how can people behave like that? At least John ... (*Looks stricken.*)

LOUISE: (*Interrupts.*) Didn't I say I was the clever one this time. No angry wife after me. Not Guilty!

KATE: (*Vaguely.*) I should hope not, bet you've had some near misses though.

LOUISE: You're not really listening to me are you? What are you cuddling that fluffy thing for? (KATE *puts it between them. Pause.*) Holy cow! Tell me you're not, you know ... Yes. I bet that's what's wrong with you. I've watched you wandering about in a dream. That's it isn't it? You're pregnant again.

KATE: (*Emphatically.*) No I'm not!

LOUISE: Well something's up with you. (*Pause.*) What was that you said about John?

KATE *looks away from her. Looks down at her hands in her lap.*

LOUISE: Hey, come on. What's getting at you? Let me fill your glass. There's just a little drop left.

KATE: No, you have it.

LOUISE: Come on tell me what's up? I might be able to help if it's to do with the kids. Give you a break if you like at the weekend. William, Sarah and Michael love playing with their auntie and I love playing with them. (*Pause.*) It's John, isn't it? You're worried about him aren't you?

KATE: In a way yes. Oh he's not ill or anything, it's just ... well (*Thoughtfully.*) I suppose I could say he's a bit like you.

LOUISE: (*Astounded.*) Like me! What like me?

KATE: Well, fancying someone. He just seems to, I don't know, fancy this woman he met at the classes.

LOUISE: Is that all? I bet you have fancies yourself. (*Laughing.*) What about Tesco's delivery bloke you was on about last week? Anyway, John's not stupid. He loves you to bits and absolutely adores the children.

KATE: I know all that. It's just the way he goes on and on. It's been Emily this and Emily that for the last two weeks. How wonderfully she speaks, how elegantly dressed she is, her figure blah, blah. It just makes me uneasy. I feel somehow inadequate, not up to what he wants in a wife. (*She looks towards the washing.*) I could just about live without him myself (*Pause.*) No, not really I couldn't, but I could never, ever forgive him if he hurt the children.

LOUISE: I can't believe I'm hearing this. You must joking. John's not daft, he wouldn't risk anything to hurt his family. The kids worship him. Are you sure about this?

KATE: What would you think if, say for instance, you knew his classes ended at nine-thirty, and then for the last two weeks he turns up just before eleven? He

	says he goes to the pub with the tutor and other people in the group, but it just bothers me somehow. What do you think?
LOUISE:	Well, as groups get friendlier they do. You know begin to socialise a bit, carry on from where the lecture ended. We did when I was at college. It happens all the time.
KATE:	But I can't bear feeling so insecure anymore. I just feel so mumsy somehow. I just feel so, so I don't know … So used, ordinary somehow. I mean I held down a damn good job, people asked for and respected my opinions. Now I have nothing adult or intellectual to talk about let alone take part in. No wonder John might be looking elsewhere. I mean, honestly I'm so boring! Aren't I? Don't answer that.
LOUISE:	Steady on Kate. You're really going through it aren't you?
KATE:	You know what I really wanted to do? I wanted to be an editor, even have my own magazine in time. And that's the fly in the ointment. Time. Flying by, and I haven't even got started. I've masses of ideas whizzing around in my head, but …
LOUISE:	Kate love, you're not thirty yet. There's plenty of time. Lots of women don't start their careers until they've gone forty or more.
KATE:	Thanks a lot! Only another eleven years to go. (*Pause. Then smartly.*) There's only one way to go. Nip this business with John in the bud now.
LOUISE:	Hey now, steady on. What are you thinking of doing?
KATE:	Still got to work that one out. You know, I'm fairly sure nothing has happened yet between them, but he wants to improve his brain, and as it's the tutor at his classes, I don't want him to think his brain is in his trousers. (*They both laugh.*) Well enough is enough. I'm not letting it get any further.

LOUISE:	Seriously Kate, do be careful.
KATE:	What do you mean? I'm not going to scratch her eyes out or anything. But I do know I've very little to fight her with.
LOUISE:	Don't say 'fight'. It reminds me what happened at school, when your date – Malcolm somebody or other – went out with Stella. You went wild in the playground. Suspended for the week if I remember.
KATE:	Oh, that was just the hormones talking!
LOUISE:	You could have fooled me! What about the time in the Juniors?
KATE:	Now what are you going to drag up?
LOUISE:	If I remember rightly, you wanted to sit next to Brian Smithers, and Becky erm. Forgot her name for a minute. Well anyway Becky got there first. You were so mad.
KATE:	I don't remember.
LOUISE:	Yes you do! You don't want to remember. (*Slyly.*) You. (*She giggles.*) You put a worm in her wellies in the cloakroom.
KATE:	(*Horrified.*) I didn't! I don't like worms!
LOUISE:	Yes you did. You made me carry the worm. (*They both laugh.*)
KATE:	(*Goes to the table and picks up a piece of paper.*) Listen, I found this on the Internet: 'Mother's glue is not a recipe or that sticky stuff used in art. It's that special love that mothers use to keep your family from falling apart.'
LOUISE:	That's lovely. Who wrote it?
KATE:	It just said Unknown. But that sums up how I feel, and that's the glue I'll use to keep us all together – mother love.

LOUISE: Promise me Kate, promise me on your life, you'll not do anything, anything dangerous or end up in a police cell or something. Promise me!

KATE: 'Course I won't! I love John too much and couldn't live without the kids and as Gilbert Keith Chesterson said, 'The way to love anything is to realise it might be lost.' So, I'll think of something and soon.

LOUISE: You and your quotations! Do you quote to John all the time? That's why he's going to classes I bet, so he can keep up with you!

KATE: (*Brighter now she seems to have made her mind up to do something.*) What John did say, was why don't you and I have an evening out. He suggested yoga, or something girlie.

LOUISE: Yes! I know the very thing! Let's go clubbing! There's a new one just opened. I'll drive then you can let your hair down.

KATE: You must be joking! Anyway, I've nothing to wear. Look at the time. Go on, clear off.

LOUISE: (*Snatches up another biscuit, and with full mouth.*)

On my way. See you next week and remember what I said, no worms or anything!! (*Leaves laughing.*)

Lights down.

Scene 2

Lights up.

In the same room a week later. The room is tidy and there are two glasses and a few poetry books on the table.

KATE has smartened herself up. A neat dress, tidy hair and make-up. She paces up and down the room obviously very anxious.

A flustered LOUISE enters. She does not look at KATE but throws her coat onto a chair looks in the mirror and fluffs up her hair.

LOUISE: I'm sorry I'm so late. Here's your keys. (*Puts them on the table.*) I expect John left them in the door for ... (*Sees glasses.*) I'm so sorry! I didn't bring a bottle. I meant too ... (*Turns and sees* KATE.) Hey! Look at you! Love your dress.

KATE: You like it? (*Gives a spin.*) Bought it before the kids were born. Lucky really I can get into it.

LOUISE: Great, that colour suits you. You should dress up more often. I meant to bring a bottle tonight as we have something to celebrate.

KATE: I could do with some good news. So, come on what is it?

LOUISE: I'll tell you in a minute because ... You remember I told you last week about Robin and his office harem! Well, you won't believe this. It seems Maggie is expecting after all! Poor cow, she's at her wits end.

KATE: And I suppose he doesn't want to know.

LOUISE:	I don't think he does know. She's like a lost soul, none of us know what to say for the best. She just cries and cries.
KATE:	Well the sooner she pulls herself together the better. She'll make herself ill otherwise.
LOUISE:	Well enough of that. Tral la la! (*She thrusts out her left hand and twirls about.*)
KATE:	You haven't! You're engaged! (*Excitedly they embrace each other.*) Congratulations. Oh a thousand congratulations.
	(*Doubtfully.*) Er … It is to George I trust?
LOUISE:	'Course it's George!
KATE:	This calls for a celebration. Do you think it's a special occasion?
LOUISE:	Definitely!
KATE:	Then I shall open one of John's special bottles! (*They both laugh.* KATE *brings out a bottle and opener. She hesitates for a moment.*)
LOUISE:	Go on. He won't mind.
KATE:	Oh yes, he probably will! Anyway he did say he was keeping it for special occasions.
	(*She pours out their drinks; sits down beside LOUISE. They raise their glasses, giggle and then quietly take a few sips.*)
LOUISE:	(*Turns to* KATE.) Now then, what's your news and why the glad rags?
KATE:	More like power dressing. You know, to boost my confidence.
LOUISE:	Whatever for?
KATE:	(*Seriously.*) To face John when he gets back from his class.
LOUISE:	It can't be that bad, anyway, you can handle him. He's like a pussycat around you.

KATE: It is bad, seriously bad and it's not something I intended to happen but, oh God, it did. (*Pause.*) You remember last week …

LOUISE: (*Shakes her head.*) Not really.

KATE: Yes you do, remember I told you about John's er … liking of that Emily something..

LOUISE: Ah! Yes, you thought it might be developing into someth … (*Aghast.*) Kate! You didn't, you didn't do anything stupid did you?

KATE: Yes and no. (*Begins to walk restlessly about the room.*) It all happened in less than, oh ten minutes at the most. I just don't know what John is going to say.

LOUISE: For heaven's sake, what happened? Come and sit down and tell me. There might be something I can do to help.

KATE: (*Sits. Pours out more wine.*) Better leave some for John, he's going to need it. And no, there's nothing on earth you can do to put this right!

LOUISE: What, just what have you done Kate?

KATE: Funny enough Lou, it wasn't me, it was the kids.

LOUISE: The kids! How?

KATE: You remember I said I was going to find a way to, well stop John falling for her and leave me and the children. (*Big sigh.*) I decided I'd go round to her house, John said where she lived, on the moneyed side of town of course. I looked up her name in the directory, Miss E. Lacey Elliot. It was quite a trek, had to change buses at the market. Thought I'd just take the children and introduce us all so that she could see … I don't know …

LOUISE: What a grand loving family he's got?

KATE: Yes, I suppose that's it exactly.

LOUISE: So what happened?

KATE: I should have allowed for the children getting excited. I mean how many times have they been on a bus? That started them off. By the time we got to the house, they were really hyped up, especially Michael. Sarah started doing cartwheels on the front lawn and landed on the flowers. (*Sighs.*) and William was chewing gum. God knows where he got that from. I did my best to get them together and tidy. (*Pause.*) Anyway, I knocked and after a little while SHE answered the door. (*Long pause.*)

LOUISE: And?

KATE: She ... (*Lifts up her hands then drops them suddenly.*) She is everything John says.

LOUISE: (*Shocked.*) What?

KATE: Honestly! She is breathtakingly beautiful, poised ... and, and so young! (*Pause.*) I absolutely gave up for a moment. I felt utterly deflated. Then I remembered what was at stake. Sarah was tugging at my coat and that helped, then one of Blake's poems came to mind.

LOUISE: Tyger! Tyger! burning bright?

KATE: No, no. not that one. The one that says something like I was angry. Hang on. (*She opens the book on the table and searches.*) Here it is. The Poison Tree. 'I was angry with my foe, I told it not, my wrath did grow.'

LOUISE: Poetry! You really are as bad as John. You've lost me.

KATE: I really was getting mad by now. So I said to her, quite nicely, Hi, I'm John's wife. Thought I'd call, wanted to meet you and introduce you to his children.

LOUISE: What did she say to that, the little madam!

KATE: She took a step back into the hallway, she was so shocked. Then she said, 'I don't understand.' And I thought, 'Oh yes you do lady.' Then she said,

'There's no way my John has a wife or children. You must be mistaken.'

LOUISE: But there was no mistake, was there? You could tell, couldn't you, by her surprise.

KATE: Oh yes! Of course, the kids weren't standing still. With ease, William wriggled his way into her hall and he called out 'A doggy mummy,' or something like that and the other two just sort of threw themselves after him to see this dog. It was a picture, by the way, on the wall.

LOUISE: Ah! That's lovely. And then what?

KATE: (*Pause.*) I waited for a bit, then called them, you know how I do in age order, William, Sarah, Michael. (*Pause.*)

LOUISE: And I keep wondering who's next!

KATE: (*Crossly.*) Very funny!

LOUISE: Sorry. Go on.

KATE: It was too late. I could see William had made for the kitchen, I couldn't see Michael. They do love to explore new places, and Sarah was crossing her legs begging for the lav.

KATE *walks about, biting her lips, crosses her arms across her chest, raises her shoulders and sighs.*

LOUISE: Well, she is only a little girl for heaven's sakes.

KATE: I called the boys again. To be honest I was secretly glad at the way things were going. Show her what it's like, chasing after three kids all day. She began sort of protesting, huffing and puffing. You could see she didn't know how to handle things. (LOUISE *leans forward, resting chin in hand, in anticipation.*) I asked if Sarah could use the bathroom. Emily what'sit didn't like the idea. You could tell she wanted us gone but she pointed up the stairs, and I stepped past her into the hall to wait so Sarah went up on her own. I asked her to bring down some tissue for Michael's nose and I heard thingy sort of gasp behind me.

LOUISE: (*Leans back.*) What's her place like?

KATE: Well, I looked around, and thought, what has John let himself in for? I mean. Just one look around the hall and I knew he could never keep up such a place on his money.

LOUISE: Posh was it?

KATE: I'll say! Fresh roses in a cut glass vase on an antique table, proper tailored curtains, parquet flooring. Everything tidy, clean and shining. Bet she has a char. Lord knows what the rest of the place was like.

LOUISE: Perhaps she's the one with the dosh?

KATE: I told her, John could never keep this place on and she said, he'd already bought it! I was flabbergasted! I remember thinking where did he get the money from? (*Pause.*) She, her, you know, just looked at me absolutely bewildered. (*Pause.*) I just don't understand. Something's wrong somewhere, I mean, where would John get that sort of money and me not knowing? (*Pause.*) I don't know ... So I added salt to her wound so to speak.

LOUISE: Oh no! Go on. What did you say?

KATE: I told her. (*Pause.*) I told her that if he leaves me he will have to take his three children, I emphasised three, as there was no way I could support them.

LOUISE: What did she say to that?

KATE: Hang on. (*Goes to door and listens.*) Just checking. They were tired out. (*Pause.*) Nothing really, but I could see she was close to tears. Anyway by now Sarah had come downstairs. (*Begins to laugh quietly.*) Oh! I shouldn't laugh really, (*Chuckles.*) but the little minx came up to me and said lovely smelly things up there mummy. Oh Lou, she was covered from head to toe in talc. (*They both laugh.*)

LOUISE: I bet you wished you had a camera. What was madam's reaction?

KATE: I heard her take a deep growly breath like this. (*Demonstrates.*) I could tell she was getting mad now, so I called the boys, as I do, William, Michael, they came running straight away bless them. (*Pause.*) And then I saw ...

LOUISE: What? Go on.

KATE: John will be so angry when he finds out. He probably knows by now.

LOUISE: What's the time? (*Both look at watches.*) Probably.

KATE: First William came, and I could see he had discarded his gum somewhere. I dread to think where. You know I don't allow them gum. Anyway he was eating an apple. So I told him what he had done was stealing and made him say sorry. Which he did. I was quite proud of him, he was so grown up about it. (*Pause.*) Then Michael came and ... I can't be sure but ...

LOUISE: What did he do?

KATE: There was some loose thread in the buckle of his sandal. Climbing about as usual I suspect and I think he must have snagged the furniture. That's what it looked like anyway.

LOUISE: (*Very slowly with awe.*) Oh my God! This is like something from that new magazine *Get Even* or something like that.

KATE: (*Smugly.*) Miss Lacey Elliott went ballistic. Striding about, stamping her foot, arms waving. Look, just like this. (*Demonstrates.*) I won't tell you what she called the children, and her supposed to be a lady! She said to get my tribe out of her house now, and threatened to call the police. In fact she began dialling. I mean, John will be mortified if it gets that far.

LOUISE:	Well … you can understand her reaction. I mean …
KATE:	I know what you mean. In my heart of hearts I really began to feel a bit sorry for her. Only a tiny bit mind.
LOUISE:	You didn't apologise did you?
KATE:	Well, I suppose, a bit half-heartedly. For heaven's sake, she's stealing my husband. Don't forget that. (*Pause. Dejected.*) I got the kids away as quickly as possible. When we reached the gate, Michael turned and you won't believe what he said.
LOUISE:	Come on, what did he say?
KATE:	He said, quite solemnly, we don't like you.
LOUISE:	(*Laughs*) That's my boy!
KATE:	Kids are so perceptive, aren't they? It was over so quickly. In less than ten minutes we were on our way home again. Thankfully no signs of the police yet, so hopefully she changed her mind. Tell you what though, she was absolutely shattered.
LOUISE:	You daft bugger, she hasn't got your address … unless John gave it to her, which I doubt seeing as she didn't know about his family.
KATE:	Oh Lou! What do you think he's is going to say … or do?
LOUISE:	If I were you, I'd be honest with him. Get him to listen to your side of the story. 'Course he's going to be angry, but I think he'll wake up now that you know and realise what he'd miss if he left you and the kids. (*Pause.*) Tell you what, I'll phone you, say in about half an hour after he gets in. That way whatever is happening …
	KATE *looks horrified.*
LOUISE:	Don't look like that, he's not going to kill you! But if he's in a temper it will cool him down a bit. Let him answer the phone and if he's obstreperous I'll lay into him myself.

KATE: All right.

          LOUISE *puts her coat on.*

KATE: You're going? I suppose it's time. My stomach is going over and over again.

LOUISE: Yes, I'll be on my way. You'll be all right, you see. Keep your spirits up. In fact, have another glass of that wine, that should set you up for whatever's in store! By the way, you look great. So for now, (*Dramatically.*) 'Good night. Good night! Parting is such sweet sorrow'. See I know some too. I haven't forgotten my GCSE English Lit Shakespeare innit!

KATE: (*Laughing.*) Bet you don't know where it's from?

LOUISE: *A Midsummer Night's Dream*?

KATE: Oh you! It's from *Romeo and Juliet*. Go on, he'll be here any minute.

LOUISE: Got you laughing though. Night, night our Kate.

          Lights down.

Scene 3

Lights up.

KATE is anxiously pacing and touching objects that make up her home while waiting for JOHN's return. KATE finds a toy and shoves it under a cushion. She hears him enter the hall and quickly puts her hands together in a quick prayer and crosses herself.

JOHN: (*Calls out cheerfully.*) Hi, anyone home? Kate? (JOHN *enters the room.*) I've brought someone home to meet you.

A smart 60ish woman, EMILY, follows him into the room. JOHN turns to her and guides her to the sofa.

JOHN: Come on in, make yourself at home.

KATE: (*Flustered.*) You're early John, earlier than I expected.

JOHN: There you are. Now, I want you to meet our tutor, Miss Emily Lacey Elliot. (*Turns to* EMILY.) And this is my wife, Kate, er ... Katherine.

KATE is stunned. KATE finds it difficult to understand what is happening. EMILY puts out her hand to shake.

EMILY: I am so pleased to meet you. Nearly always, John's second word is 'Kate'.

KATE: (*Rubs her hand down her skirt. Extends it to* EMILY.) Oh! Er, I wasn't expecting anyone this evening. (*Hurriedly.*) Except my sister of course, she comes every week when John is at his classes. How do you do?

JOHN:	Thought you'd be surprised! Can you rustle up some nibbles and I'll open a bottle. (*Sees one of his precious wines on the table. Lifts and turns sharply to* KATE.)
KATE:	(*Anxious to avoid a scene.*) I'll see what there is, but tomorrow is my shop day, so don't expect much. EMILY *smiles understandingly.*
JOHN:	(*Intercepts* KATE *at the door and hisses out of* EMILY*'s hearing.*) You've opened it. I've been saving that, it's nearly eight years old. What do you think you're up to?
KATE:	(*Loud whisper.*) You said it was for a special occasion and ...
JOHN:	(*Loud whisper.*) Yes! but not for you and your sister to swallow willy-nilly, just on a whim!
KATE:	As far as we're concerned it was, is a special occasion. Lou has ...
JOHN:	Nothing you two get up to could justify opening that bottle. Nothing, and I'm really pissed off.
EMILY:	Everything alright? I wonder if I might use the bathroom Kate?
JOHN:	(*Pleasantly.*) Yes, yes of course. First on left upstairs, and Kate, see what you can find. Cheese and biscuits will do fine.
EMILY:	(*As she leaves the room.*) I always find cheese goes very well with whatever wine, be it supermarket plonk or your very best vintage.
KATE:	I'm not very hopeful, but I'll see what I've got. (JOHN *and* KATE *are now alone.* KATE *rounds on* JOHN *and prods him forcefully in the chest.*) You bastard! I don't know if you've been winding me up or you are just plain insensitive.
JOHN:	What? What have I done now?

KATE: You know damn well. You've put me through hell these last few weeks. Making out Emily was the woman in your life.

JOHN: I never. I just said how good she looked.

KATE: Yes! She's everything you said, but you omitted one important fact.

JOHN: What?

KATE: Her age John! How do you think I felt when you were praising her to the high heavens. (*Walks about the room.*) God! I'm so embarrassed. and you don't know the half of it ... (*Stands defiantly in front of JOHN.*) I've had enough John. There's going to be some changes around here. For a start, you can have the kids on Saturday. I'm off for a bit of retail therapy. EARLY, so you will have to give them breakfast, lunch and their supper. I shall expect them bathed and ready for bed when I get back. (*Pause. Thoughtfully.*) I think I'll have a new outfit, something young and perhaps a little daring. Yes, then when Lou asks me to go clubbing next time, I'll be ready.

JOHN: Steady on Kate. I don't mind looking after the kids while you go window shopping, but I work all week I should have some time to rest up.

KATE: And you don't think I work all week! You go out eight o'clock, fed, sandwiches ready, home to a good hot meal, feet up watching tele. Oh I nearly forgot, you have to struggle off to Adult Education on Thursdays. Shall I begin to tell you of my days? – they are twenty-four hours long.

JOHN: Aw, come on Kate. This isn't like you. I didn't know I'd upset you so much. I'm sorry. (*Pause.*) Perhaps we could all could come with you on Saturday?

KATE: No John. I need some time for myself.

EMILY *returns.*

KATE: (*Turns to her adjusts her tone.*) Right, I'm just off to see what I can rustle up Emily. Can't promise anything, but there's sure to be something.

KATE *leaves the room.* EMILY *sits down.*

EMILY: You're so lucky John, a lovely wife, and is it three children?

JOHN: Yes, three, two boys William and Michael and a girl, Sarah, the youngest. And Kate, love of my life, (*Laughs.*) before poetry of course.

EMILY: I suppose you have a modern sort of marriage, Share all the responsibilities.

JOHN: Well, er, we, (*Brightly.*) Well for instance Kate's going out for the day on Saturday so it's my turn to look after the children.

EMILY: Seems to be the natural thing to do these days. Share responsibilities. I just couldn't give up my career myself. Become all domesticated, I mean. That was quite normal in those days. Women quite accepted their role. Thank God for modern marriages I say. (*Thoughtfully.*) Of course I regret not having a family of my own. I can see Kate takes it all in her stride though.

KATE *enters carrying a tray.*

JOHN: (*Goes to help her.*) Heavens Kate, you can't dish up that with this wine!

KATE: Why not? I cut what's left of the cheese into bite sizes and ...

JOHN: You just can't eat jammy dodgers with wine!

KATE: If they're good enough for my sister they're ...

EMILY: Jammy dodgers! Haven't had those, oh, since all my nephews and nieces grew up. We used to eat them by the ton. Love them. Bring them over Kate, I'll be able to relive my past!! I just love that chewy bit in the middle.

	JOHN *gets out extra glass and pours the wine.* KATE *passes out plates and offers the tray of eats. The telephone rings. Nobody moves.*
JOHN:	(*Reluctantly goes to answer it.*) I'll answer it shall I? Can't think who it can be?
	JOHN *remains on the phone.* EMILY *and* KATE *talk.*
EMILY:	Yes, as I was saying Kate, my brothers all had families. I remained single, as I was telling John but I enjoyed being auntie to them all. My last niece is getting married shortly. Named after me, Emily Lacey Elliot, not for much longer though, soon to be Mrs Emily Bannister Jones. Lives close by.
	KATE *looks embarrassed, fidgets, looks towards* JOHN *anxiously.*
KATE:	(*Weakly.*) Yours is certainly an unusual name.
EMILY:	Yes it is isn't it? We live in the same street, and I often get her mail and sometimes her telephone calls.
KATE:	Oh!
EMILY:	Got over that by getting myself a mobile.
	EMILY *fishes in her bag and flourishes phone.* JOHN *returns to them.*
JOHN:	(*Indignantly.*) You didn't tell me Lou has got herself attached to George at last!
KATE:	I did try John, when you went on about opening the wine for special occasions.
EMILY:	Engaged? That your sister Kate? (*Turns to* JOHN.) I was just telling Kate about my niece, she's engaged and I used to get her calls. But I must tell you this, she telephoned me this afternoon. Absolutely beside herself. She …
KATE:	(*Interrupts quickly.*) What were the poems you all discussed this evening John?

JOHN: (*Bewildered by the obvious attempt at changing the conversation.*) Er? What? What were you saying Emily?

EMILY: Relationships, you know, fathers and sons, daughters and fathers that sort of thing. As I was saying ...

KATE: (*Weakly.*) Oh, quite interesting.

EMILY: Well, first time round it was but after so many years ... Anyway as I was saying, Em phoned me this afternoon, very upset almost hysterical. Had quite a job to quieten her down. (*Sips her wine.*)

             This is lovely wine, John.

             KATE *begins to walk about agitatedly.*

JOHN: Come and sit down Kate.

             KATE *stays well away from them wringing her hands.*

EMILY: Seems a frumpy young woman with an unruly mob of children, her words exactly ...

KATE: (*Whispers.*) I'm not fr... (*Then stops.*)

EMILY: (*Glances at* KATE *and smiles.*) ... called saying they were John's. John is her fiancé's name by the way, (*Glances at* JOHN.) same as yours. Anyway, the children ran all over the house, fortunately no real damage was done. Snagged the material on the sofa, spilt some talc. That sort of thing. They've worked so hard getting things together. Beginning to look like a home already.

KATE: (*Sighs with relief.*) Thank goodness for that. Was it raining when you came in John?

JOHN: Don't think so. (*Bewildered by* Kate's question. *Gets another bottle out and waves it the women.*) More wine Emily? Kate?

EMILY: (*Stretches out her legs, relaxes.*) That would be lovely.

JOHN *pours out wine.*

EMILY: When my brothers and myself discovered the joys of a glass of wine, my grandfather used to recite a little poem. Let me think. How did it go now? (*Pause.*) I remember, something like this:
　　Not drunk is he who from the floor
　　Can rise alone and still drink more;
　　But drunk is he who prostrate lies
　　Without the power to move or rise.

Laughter all round, but KATE's *laugh is nervous.*

JOHN: Who wrote that I wonder?

EMILY: There you are John, think of finding the answer as your homework, probably 18th century. Although we laughed at grandpa, he was very solemn when he quoted it to us. (*More laughter.*)

Where was I? Oh yes, Em's call this afternoon. So ... yes, so then the poor woman, demented Em says, wanted to get away so she started calling the children's names, William, Michael, Sarah and ...

JOHN: (*Gasps, then walks across to stricken* KATE. *Gently.*) Kate?

EMILY: (*Realises situation.*) Oh dear. Dear Kate. I'm so sorry. I ...

JOHN: (*Reaches out for* KATE *and holds her protectively. Quietly.*) Kate? Kate, darling, what have I done. I'm so sorry. You must have been in such a turmoil. I'm a thoughtless brute. (*Kisses her softly.*) You're right. There will be some changes around here.

KATE: Oh God! (*Pause.*) Surely Shakespeare has something profound to say about this. (*Pause.*) I know ... "Though this be madness, yet there is method in''t."

EMILY: Ah Kate, from *Hamlet*, I believe, but methinks *Love's Labour Lost*?

ALL begin to laugh.

JOHN: And Kate, how about, "But love is blind, and lovers cannot see". That just about sums up the both of us, I think.

EMILY: Straight from the *Merchant of Venice*; so there you are Kate, all sorted.

ALL *laughing and* KATE *and* JOHN *embrace.*

Lights down.

www.ingramcontent.com/pod-product-compliance
Lightning Source LLC
La Vergne TN
LVHW051713080426
835511LV00017B/2892